Why did dinosaurs become extinct?

Contents

Written by Claire Llewellyn

Collins

1 Planet dinosaur

Long ago, in the ancient past, huge **reptiles** called dinosaurs lived on Earth. They lived on our planet for over 180 million years. There were hundreds of different kinds of dinosaur. They looked different from one another and they lived in different ways. Some dinosaurs lived in forests; others stayed near water. Some dinosaurs lived alone; others in packs. Some dinosaurs ate plants; others hunted for meat.

Diplodocus was a long-necked giant that plodded along on four legs.

Compsognathus was a fast-moving, turkey-sized dinosaur.

Then, quite suddenly, about 66 million years ago, dinosaurs became **extinct**. They simply disappeared. What might have happened to them? Why did they disappear?

Did you know?

So far, about 700 different kinds of dinosaur have been identified.

Allosaurus was a two-legged, powerful hunter.

How do we learn about dinosaurs?

It's not easy to find out about animals that lived so long ago. Scientists can't go back in a time machine to see what was happening then. Everything they know about dinosaurs comes from fossils. These are the traces of ancient animals found in rocks.

How a fossil forms

After a dinosaur dies, the soft parts of its body rot away.

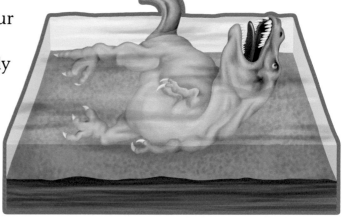

Its bones are covered by a thick layer of mud.

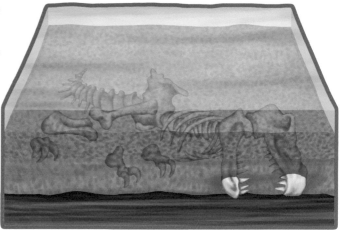

Over millions of
years, heavy
layers of mud
and sand
build up
on top.
They harden
into rock.

Water seeps into
the bones
and, slowly,
they change
into stone.

Over time, the rocks are worn
away by water, wind and ice.

Parts of the fossil can
now be seen,
and sometimes
someone finds it.

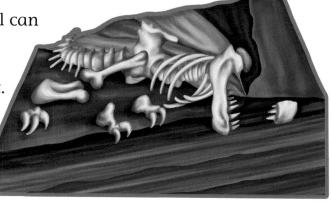

What can fossils tell us?

A dinosaur fossil provides scientists with **evidence** about life in the distant past. They study every fossil carefully. They want to know when the dinosaur was alive. Can you think how they might do this?

Using special instruments, scientists test the rock where the fossil was found. This helps them to discover its age. If the rock is 150 million years old, then any fossil found in that rock is the same age.

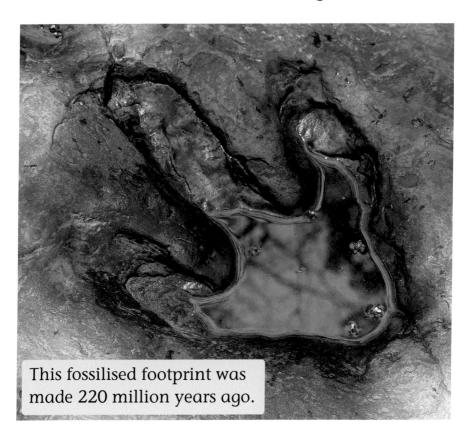

This fossilised footprint was made 220 million years ago.

Fossils often reveal the size of an animal and how it moved or ate. By comparing fossils from different times, experts can see how **species** slowly changed to suit their surroundings.

The fossilised jaw of the meat-eating Allosaurus. Unlike plant-eaters, it had long, sharp teeth.

Did you know?
Scientists have found fossils of skeletons, eggs, footprints – and even dinosaur poo!

2 Age of the Dinosaurs

Thanks to all the fossil discoveries, scientists know when dinosaurs first appeared on Earth and when they disappeared. They call this the Age of the Dinosaurs. It is split into three different periods of time called eras.

The first part is called the Triassic era. This is when the first dinosaurs appeared, such as the Postosuchus.

Postosuchus

252–201 million years ago	201–145 million years ago

Next came the Jurassic era. Stegosaurus, Apatosaurus and many other dinosaurs appeared then.

Stegosaurus

The Cretaceous era saw a huge variety of dinosaur species, such as Maiasaura and Oviraptor. Dinosaurs ruled Earth until they suddenly became extinct.

Oviraptor

Did you know?

The human story is short compared to the dinosaurs'. Our first **ancestor** appeared about six million years ago, while the first dinosaurs appeared 250 millions years ago.

now!

145-66 million years ago

Great survivors

During the Age of the Dinosaurs, there were huge changes on Earth.

In the Triassic era, all the land was joined together in one big piece. The **climate** was warm and dry. Later, **volcanoes erupted** for thousands of years, sending out deadly gases.

During the Jurassic era, the land began to split up and slowly move apart. New mountains rose up from the seabed. The climate grew warm and sticky. **Lush** forests appeared.

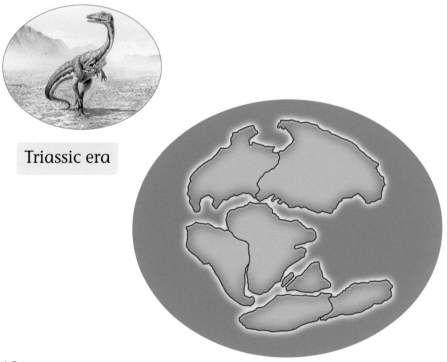

Triassic era

In the Cretaceous era, Earth's **continents** looked like they do today. The climate changed from very warm to much cooler and damper. Flowering plants appeared.

The changes must have made life difficult, and yet the dinosaurs managed to survive them all. So, what could it have been that eventually wiped them out?

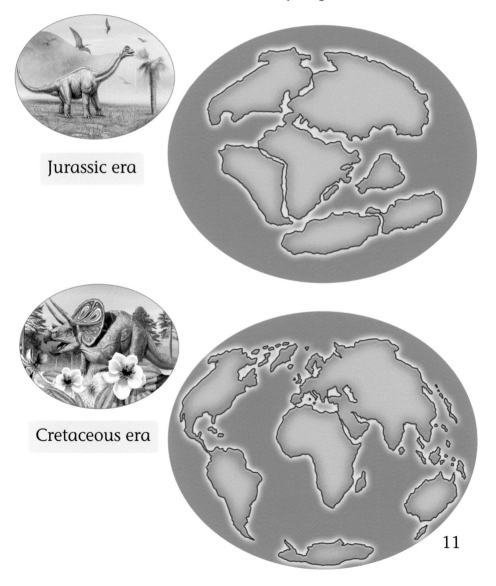

Jurassic era

Cretaceous era

3 What caused the extinction of the dinosaurs?

At the end of the Cretaceous era,
the dinosaurs disappeared. Of course, some species
had already died out. Extinction is a natural
process but it's usually very slow. The extinction of
the dinosaurs was different. They disappeared quite
rapidly and all at the same time. How do scientists
know this?

The answer is simple: scientists have never found
a dinosaur fossil in any rock younger than 66 million
years old. Something devastating must have happened
at that point. After that, there is nothing.

Many species have become extinct throughout history.

Did you know?
When lots of
species disappear
at once, it is called
a mass extinction.

Ankylosaurus was one of the last
dinosaurs to walk on Earth.

4 A prehistoric puzzle

It was about 150 years ago that scientists widely understood that the dinosaurs had disappeared in a mass extinction. The scientists had no idea what could have caused it. Fossils are the only evidence they have, and fossils are patchy: they certainly don't tell the whole story. What else can scientists do to try and solve this **prehistoric** puzzle?

They look at the evidence in fossils and rocks.

They read, study and discuss the work of many different scientific experts.

They consider animals alive today. Animals can give important clues about animal life in the past.

They think hard until they come up with a possible idea.

Finally, they try to convince other scientists that their idea is right!

5 Extinction ideas

Scientists have put forward many ideas about why the dinosaurs became extinct. Here are a number of them. Do you think they sound reasonable?

Idea one:

Dinosaurs put all their energy into growing big and spiky. This left them too **sluggish** to **adapt** to changes in the climate.

Idea two:

The shells of dinosaur eggs became too thin so they broke before hatching.

Idea three:

The shells of eggs became too thick so air couldn't get inside, and the baby dinosaurs died.

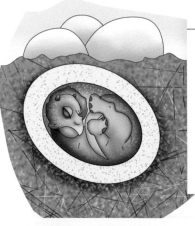

Idea four:

Earth was overrun by caterpillars.
They ate so many plants that the dinosaurs starved.

Idea five:

Strong sunlight and a hotter climate made young dinosaurs go blind. They couldn't find a mate and had no young.

Idea six:

Mammals ate all
the dinosaur eggs.

Idea seven:

Flowering plants appeared
and made lots of **pollen**.
This caused the dinosaurs to
die of **hay fever**.

Idea eight:

Changes to Earth's
climate caused heavy
rain and flooding.
All the dinosaurs drowned.

Idea nine:

The climate became too hot. This made the dinosaurs overheat, and killed off their young.

Idea ten:

Earth's climate became too cold. Dinosaurs couldn't keep warm and their eggs failed to hatch.

Do you think any of these ideas could be right?

6 Weighing up the evidence

There is little or no evidence for most of the ideas
suggested by scientists. Of course, some of the ideas
are not completely wrong. It's true that mammals
did steal dinosaur eggs, that flowering plants did
develop in the Cretaceous era, and that the climate
was unstable. But these ideas don't explain why
the dinosaurs died out so quickly.

Perhaps we should consider these questions:

- Did the dinosaurs fail to adapt in some way?
- Did climate change kill off plants that the dinosaurs relied on for food?
- Or was there some other kind of unexpected disaster?

What do you think about each of these questions?

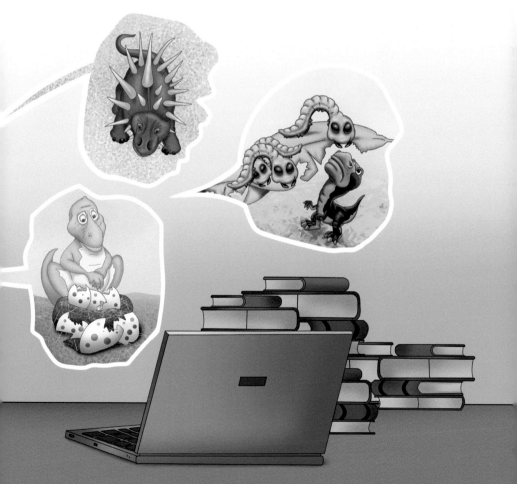

7 A new discovery

In 1980, two **geologists** called Luis and Walter Alvarez came up with a new idea. They suggested that a huge asteroid, a rock from space, crashed into Earth about 66 million years ago. It would have brought disaster for the dinosaurs.

This surprising idea came from a discovery the two scientists had made worldwide. In rocks that were 66 million years old, they had found a layer of metallic dust. The metal, called **iridium**, is very rare on Earth but common in asteroids. So how did the dust get there?

Luis and Walter suggested that it had settled all over Earth after a massive asteroid strike. So, perhaps it was an asteroid that killed off the dinosaurs? Let's find out more …

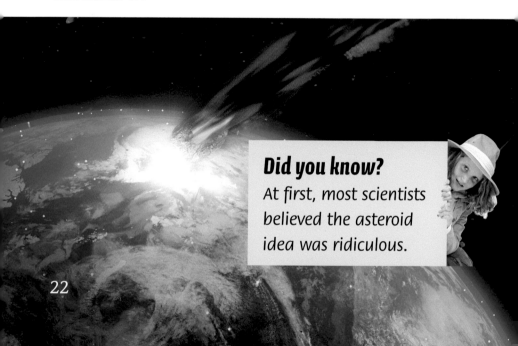

Did you know?
At first, most scientists believed the asteroid idea was ridiculous.

Luis and Walter Alvarez suggested that an asteroid strike could have spread iridium dust around the world.

Iridium is a metal rarely found on Earth.

The missing crater

Imagine an asteroid the size of a mountain rushing towards our planet. It's moving 20 times faster than a bullet. Now imagine the powerful crash as it hits Earth. It would make a massive impact, resulting in a **crater**. So, where was this crater? In 1980, no such crater had ever been found. Luis and Walter believed that one day it would be.

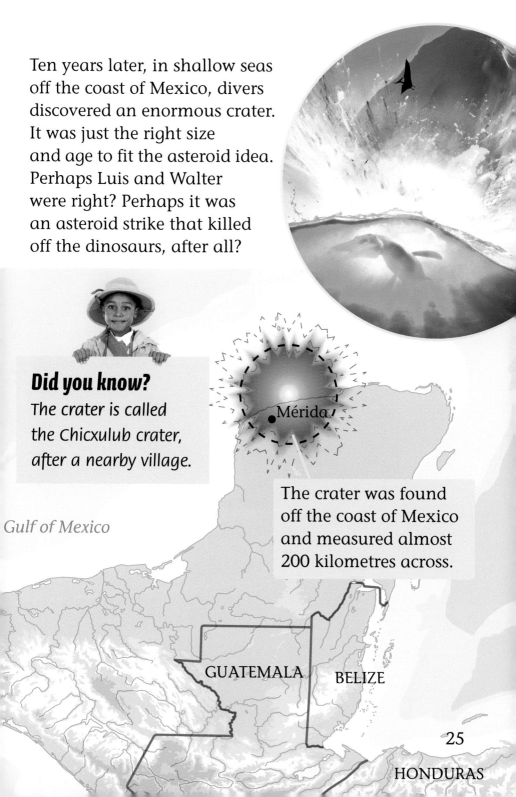

Ten years later, in shallow seas off the coast of Mexico, divers discovered an enormous crater. It was just the right size and age to fit the asteroid idea. Perhaps Luis and Walter were right? Perhaps it was an asteroid strike that killed off the dinosaurs, after all?

Did you know?
The crater is called the Chicxulub crater, after a nearby village.

Mérida

Gulf of Mexico

The crater was found off the coast of Mexico and measured almost 200 kilometres across.

GUATEMALA

BELIZE

25

HONDURAS

The asteroid strike

Scientists have thought carefully about what might have happened to Earth 66 million years ago, after an asteroid slammed into the surface of the planet.

1 The asteroid would have blasted a deep hole in Earth's crust, sending **shockwaves** out through the rocks.

Did you know?

Scientists have estimated that the asteroid must have been at least 11 kilometres wide – that's the length of about 110 football fields.

2 Rock dust would have shot up high into the sky.

3 Massive waves would have formed in the ocean and rolled towards the coast. This would have caused flooding far inland.

All this would have killed many dinosaurs, but would it have made them extinct?

The unfolding disaster

It's almost impossible to fully grasp the power of a large asteroid strike. It would be like thousands of bombs all exploding in the same place.

The blast would have created fast-moving fireballs. Wildfires would have blazed around the world, torching the land and all its wildlife.

The shockwaves from the impact would have caused **hurricane**-strength winds, violent **earthquakes** and volcanic eruptions. These would have caused catastrophes around the world.

Many dinosaurs would have died as a result of all this, but would it have ended the Age of the Dinosaurs? They had proved themselves to be great survivors; would these events really have caused a mass extinction?

Perhaps the real killer was something else.

The cloud of dust

What would have happened to all the dust thrown up by the blast? Millions of tonnes of rocky dust would have risen high up in the sky, many kilometres above the ground. It would have formed a thick black cloud. What would have happened then?

For several days after the strike, the cloud would have grown bigger and thicker. Soon winds would have blown it around Earth. The black dust would have blocked out the Sun's rays all around the world. There would have been no heat or light on the surface of Earth. What would this mean for animals and plants?

Did you know?

An asteroid strike would cause so much dust that it would take years to settle.

A long winter

Living things would have faced a long, cold, dark winter. This would have quickly killed off the plants. All plants need light to survive, and plants then were used to a warm climate.

With nothing to eat, plant-eating dinosaurs, such as Iguanodon, would soon have starved.

Meat-eating dinosaurs, such as Tyrannosaurus rex, would have fed on their corpses. But, when the food ran out, they too would have died.

Every living species, not just the dinosaurs, would have battled to survive. Sadly, many of them disappeared for good.

Did you know?
After the asteroid strike, temperatures would have fallen rapidly, from very warm to freezing cold.

33

8 The last straw?

At the time of their extinction, dinosaurs had been around for 180 million years. They had already survived huge changes. Why didn't they survive this one?

Scientists wonder if there was an extra cause. 66 million years ago, massive volcanoes were erupting in what is now India. Of course, dinosaurs had survived volcanoes, but these were immense and went on erupting for 750,000 years. The **molten** rock they threw out formed hills three times larger than France!

These hills in India were formed by volcanoes before the dinosaurs disappeared.

Did the ash and gas from these volcanoes change Earth's climate before the asteroid? Did plants grow badly as a result? If so, this could have weakened the dinosaurs. Perhaps, when the asteroid struck, they were unable to cope.

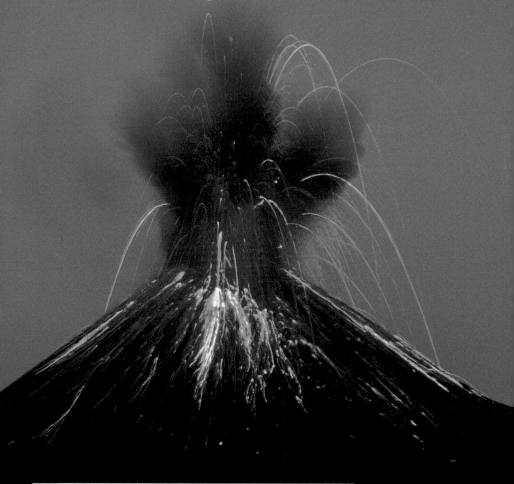

When a volcano erupts, it hurls out poisonous gases, ash and red-hot rock.

9 Not just the dinosaurs

Many animals besides the dinosaurs died out during the mass extinction. Huge sea reptiles, such as plesiosaurs, and large flying reptiles called pterosaurs both disappeared. Three-quarters of all the species that scientists know were living at the time vanished from Earth.

SURVIVED: DRAGONFLY

DIED OUT: PLESIOSAUR

DIED OUT: AMMONITE

Amazingly, some animals survived the disaster. Mammals, insects, lizards, crocodiles, turtles, birds, fish, crabs and snails all came through. How did they do it? Scientists aren't sure. Many of the animals were small so perhaps they didn't need much food. Some could burrow underground where it may have been safer. Others could swim or fly. Maybe that helped them to survive.

SURVIVED: CROCODILE

DIED OUT: PTEROSAUR

Did you know?
Very few land animals heavier than a big dog survived the disaster.

SURVIVED: FISH

10 Life returns

In time, the dust settled, warmth and sunlight reappeared, and Earth began to recover. Life grew easier for the surviving plants and animals. Mammals, in particular, now began to thrive. Up until the mass extinction, most mammals were fairly small and only came out at night. After the dinosaurs were gone, they came out during the day. They felt safer now.

Little by little, over millions of years, new mammal species began to **evolve**. Mammals became larger, and some of them began to live in the sea and the air.

After the mass extinction, bats began to evolve. Over time, they developed wings and began to fly.

50 million years ago, whales began to evolve from mammals that lived on land. Eventually, whales took to the sea.

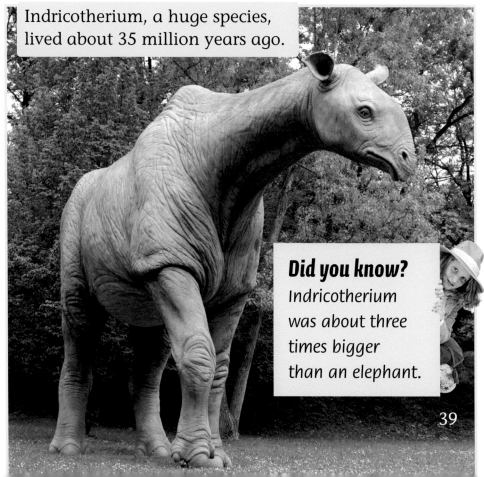

Indricotherium, a huge species, lived about 35 million years ago.

Did you know?
Indricotherium was about three times bigger than an elephant.

11 Did all the dinosaurs die?

So, did every single dinosaur disappear? No.
One group of dinosaurs was very lucky. It somehow
survived the asteroid strike, the volcanoes
and the changing climate. These dinosaurs were
smaller species and they had feathery skins.
So, what happened to them?

Feathered dinosaurs like
Microraptor were the direct
ancestors of birds.

During the next 66 million years, this group of
animals expanded and evolved. Slowly, they became
the birds we know today.

Archaeopteryx was a feathered dinosaur. Traces of its feathers can be seen in the rock.

Did you know?
Chickens, ducks and pigeons are directly related to Tyrannosaurus rex!

12 The questions continue

So, why did the dinosaurs become extinct? Scientists have suggested many reasons.

Most experts now accept that an asteroid strike killed off the dinosaurs. However, there were probably other causes, too: changes in Earth's climate, plant loss, and violent volcanoes poisoning the air. All of these would have weakened the dinosaurs before the asteroid struck.

Did you know?
It's rare for an asteroid to strike a planet: it might happen once in 100 million years.

The dinosaurs were very unlucky. If it had not been for the asteroid, they might still be alive on Earth today. How would we have shared the world with them? What do you think?

Glossary

adapt to change in order to become more successful

ancestor an animal from the past that a living animal has developed from

climate the sort of weather places normally have

continents the seven large landmasses on Earth

crater a large, bowl-shaped hollow in the ground

earthquakes the sudden shaking of the earth

erupted (a volcano) threw out fire, ash and gas

evidence information or objects that are used to prove whether something is true or not

evolve to develop slowly over time

extinct to die out and disappear from Earth

geologists people who study the history of Earth through its rocks and soil

hay fever a bad reaction to pollen that causes sneezing and itchy eyes

hurricane a tropical storm with strong winds and heavy rain

iridium a rare, hard, silver-white metal often found in asteroids

lush with lots of green, healthy plants

molten melted

pollen the yellow dust made by flowering plants that helps them to develop seeds

prehistoric about Earth's distant history, before written records

reptiles egg-laying animals with scaly skin

shockwaves energy from one spot moving and shaking the area around it

sluggish slow-moving; lacking energy

species a distinct kind of animal or plant

volcanoes holes in Earth's crust where fire, ash and gas can escape

Index

Dinosaur extinction timeline

Multiple volcanic eruptions

Plants died

Asteroid hits Earth

Dust cloud blocks the Sun

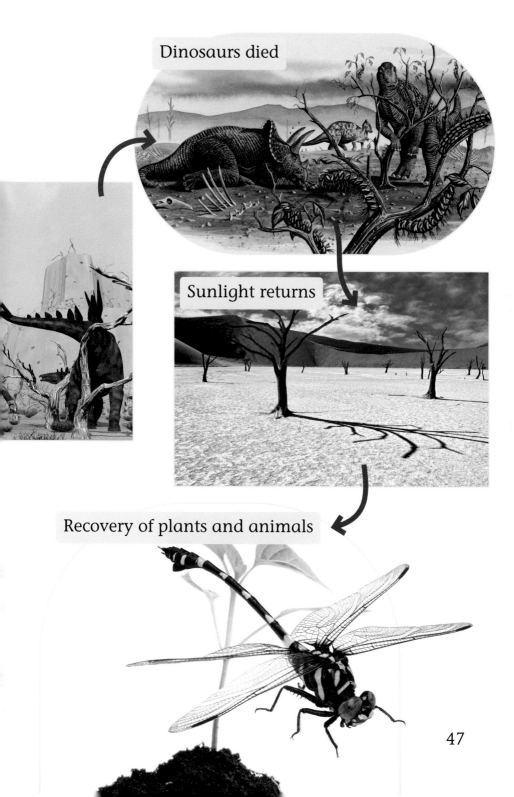

Dinosaurs died

Sunlight returns

Recovery of plants and animals

47

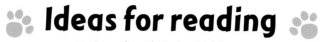 Ideas for reading

Written by Christine Whitney
Primary Literacy Consultant

Reading objectives:
- be introduced to non-fiction books that are structured in different ways
- listen to, discuss and express views about non-fiction
- retrieve and record information from non-fiction
- discuss and clarify the meanings of words

Spoken language objectives:
- participate in discussion
- speculate, hypothesise, imagine and explore ideas through talk
- ask relevant questions

Curriculum links: History: Develop an awareness of the past; Writing: Write for different purposes

Word count: 2920

Interest words: evidence, geologists, prehistoric, extinct, crater

Resources: Paper, pencils and crayons, access to the internet

Build a context for reading

- Ask children to name as many dinosaurs as they can.
- Before the children see the book, ask them what they already know about dinosaurs. Have they read any books about them? Seen any films? Visited any exhibitions?
- Now turn to the book and read the blurb on the back cover. Ask children what they understand by the word *extinct*.
- Challenge the group to give their own explanations as to *why and how such powerful reptiles* became *extinct so suddenly*.

Understand and apply reading strategies

- Turn to the contents page and read through the different sections in the book. Ask for volunteers to say which section they are most interested in reading and why.
- Read together up to page 7. Ask children to summarise what they know about how fossils are formed.